Teresa's Fantastical Whimsical Coloring Book

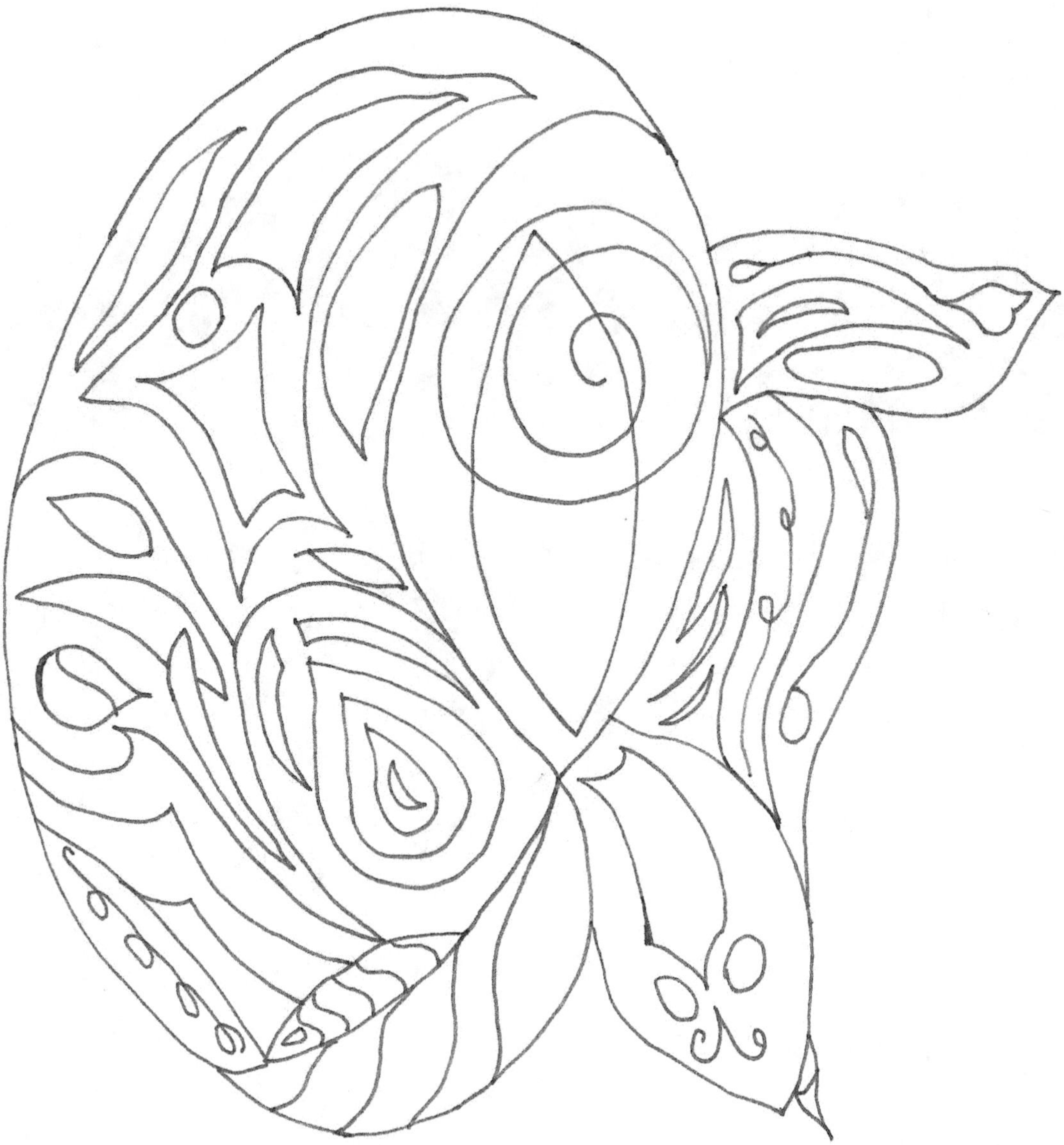

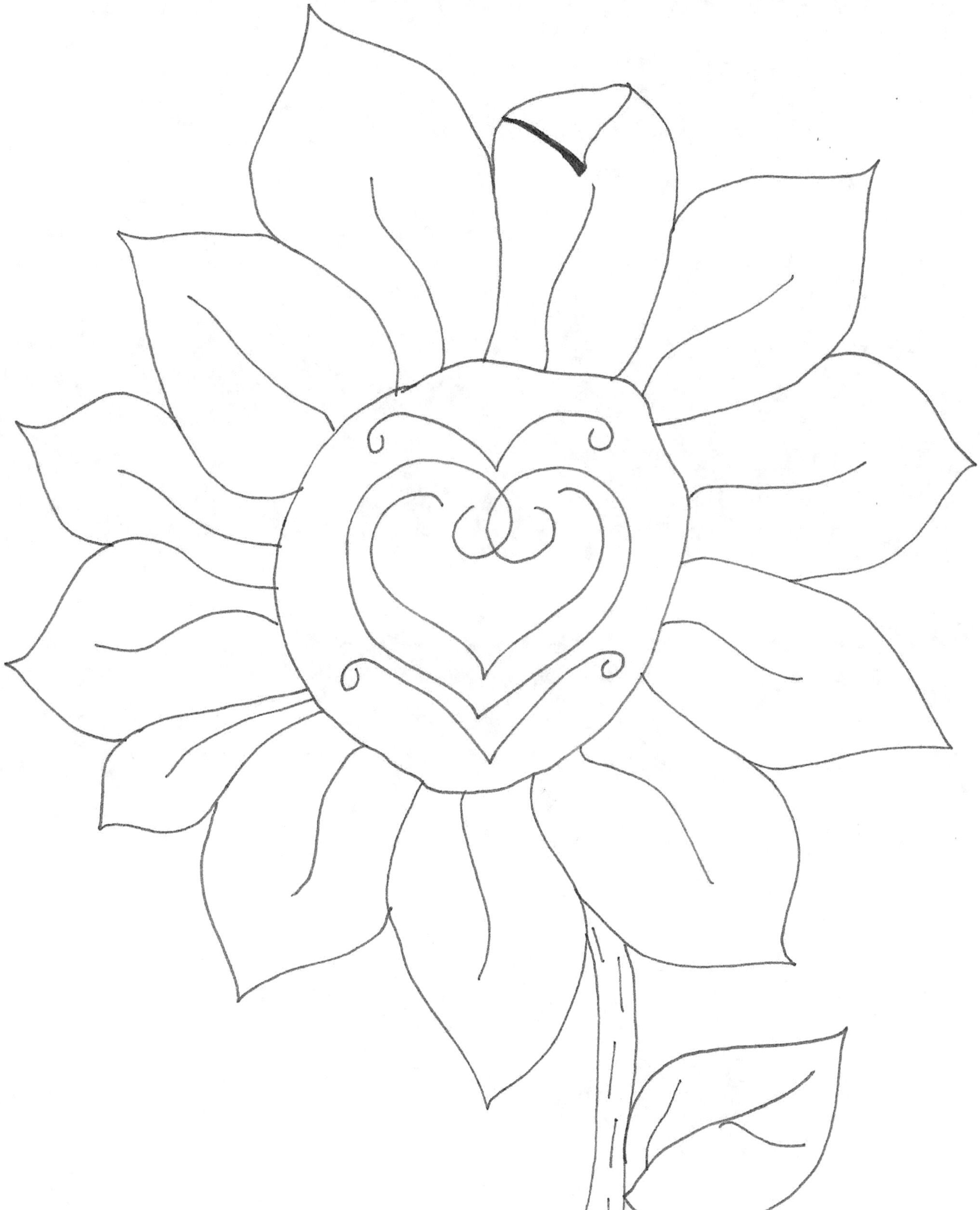

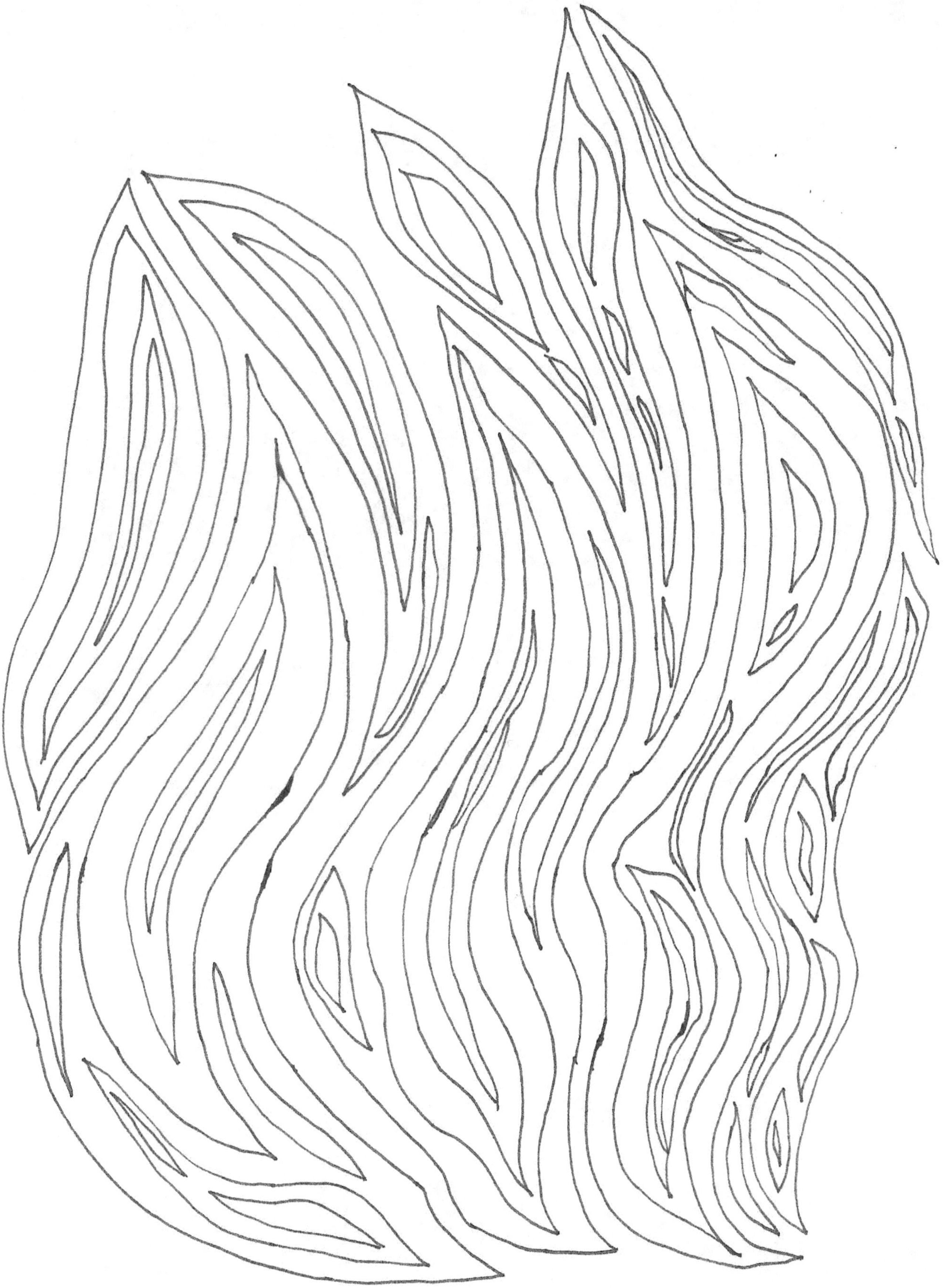

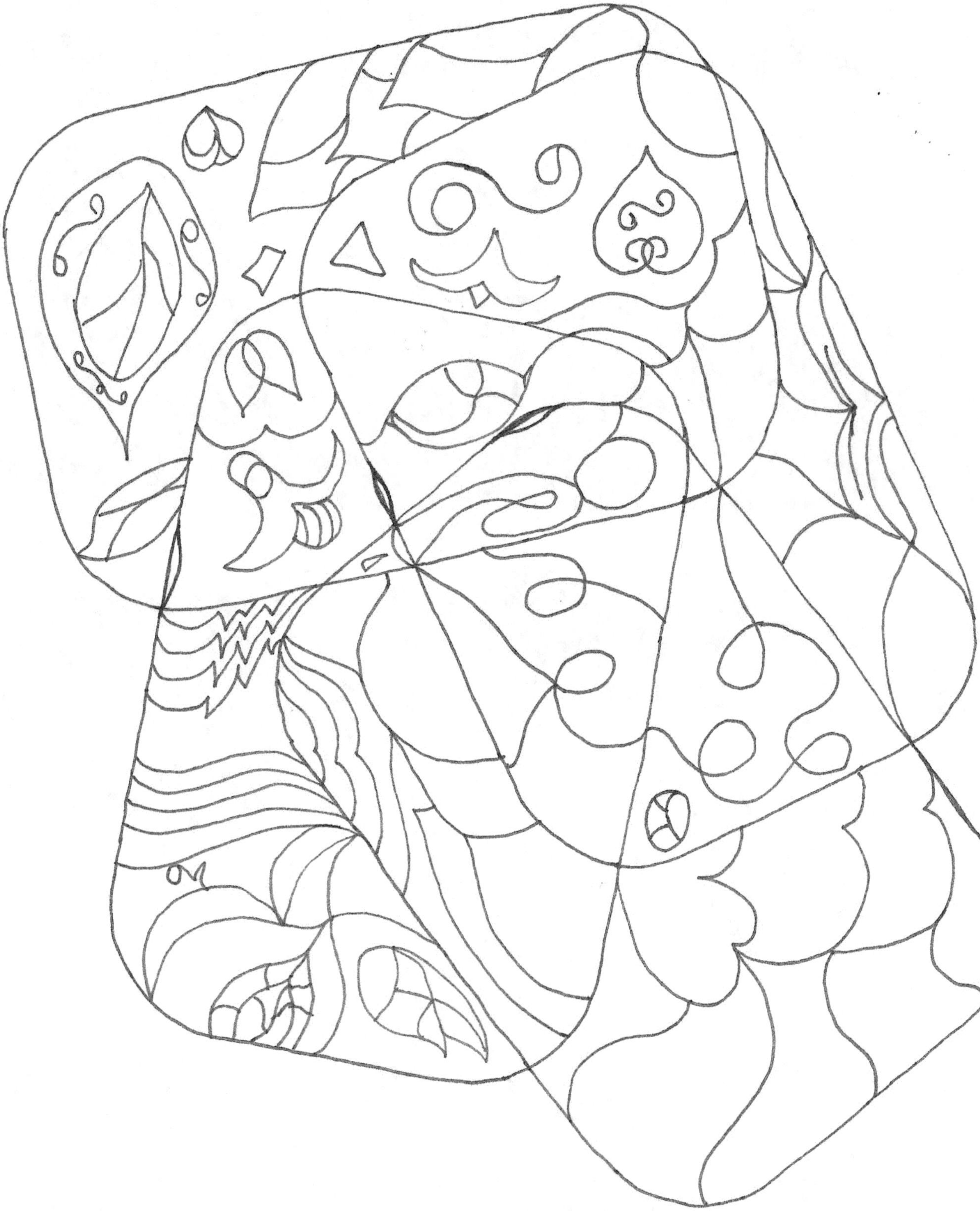

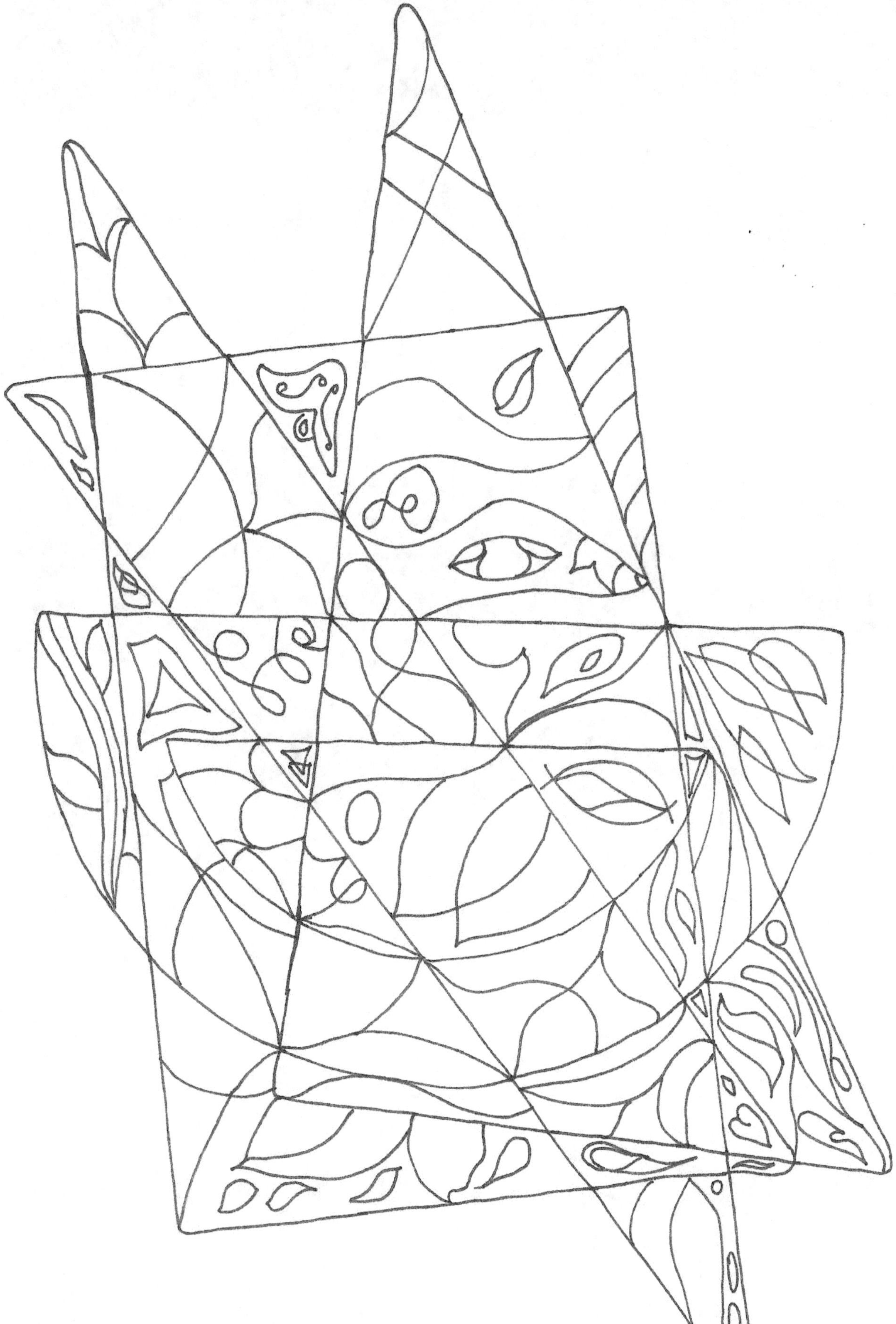

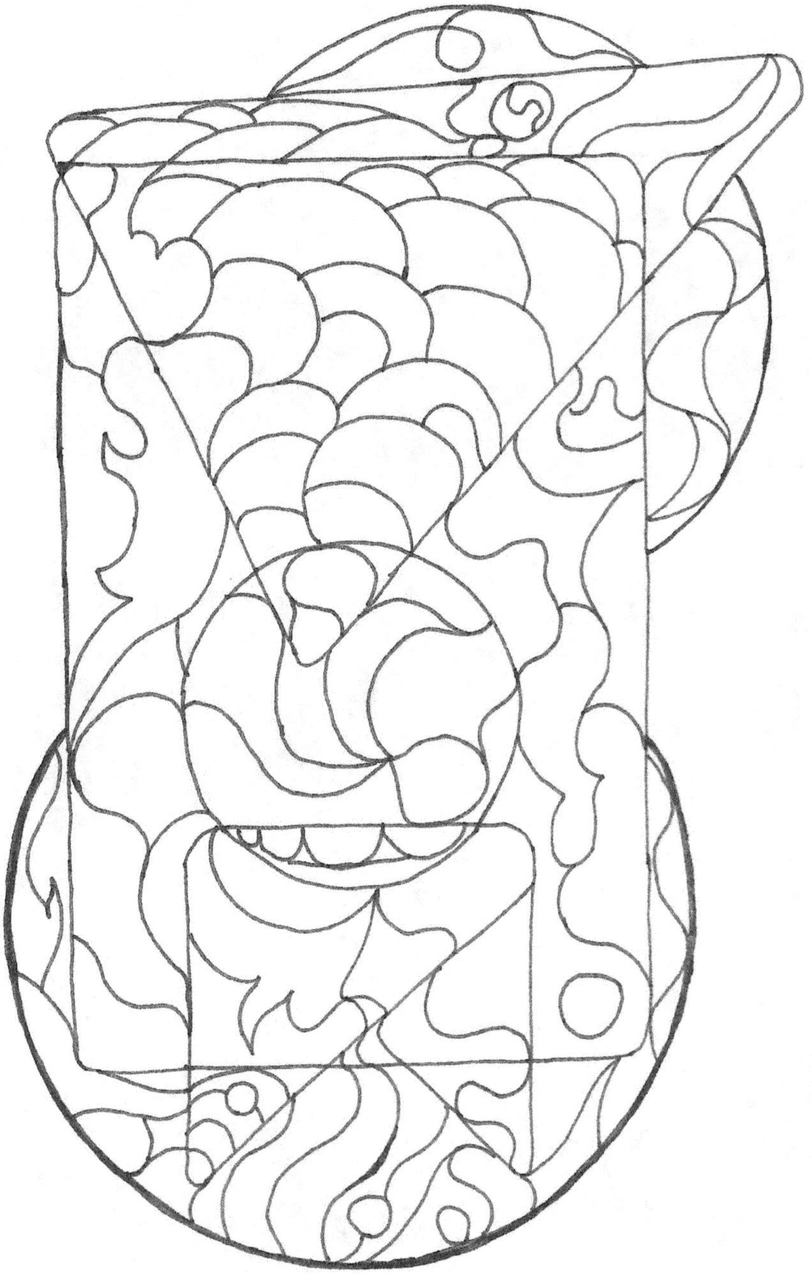

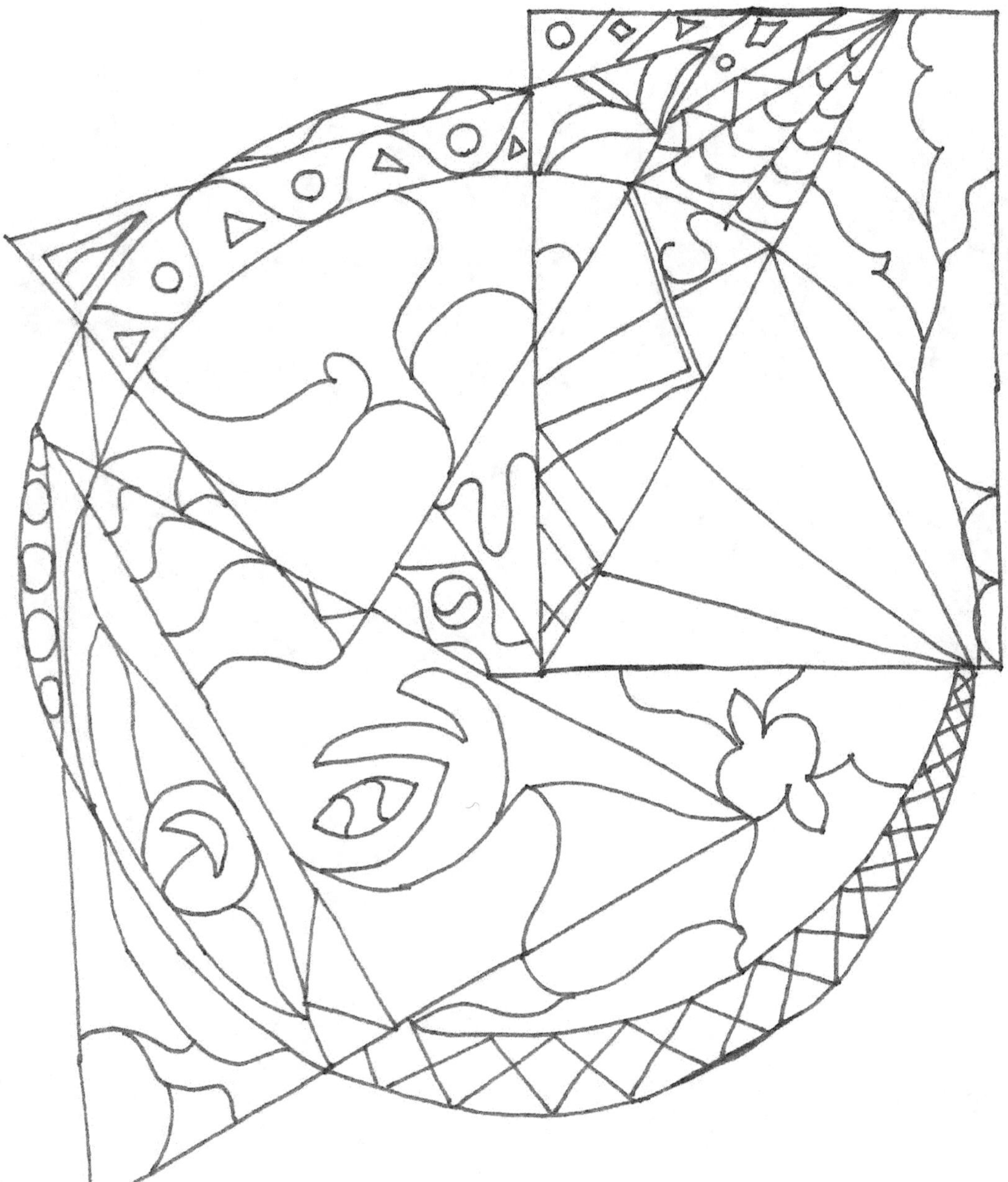

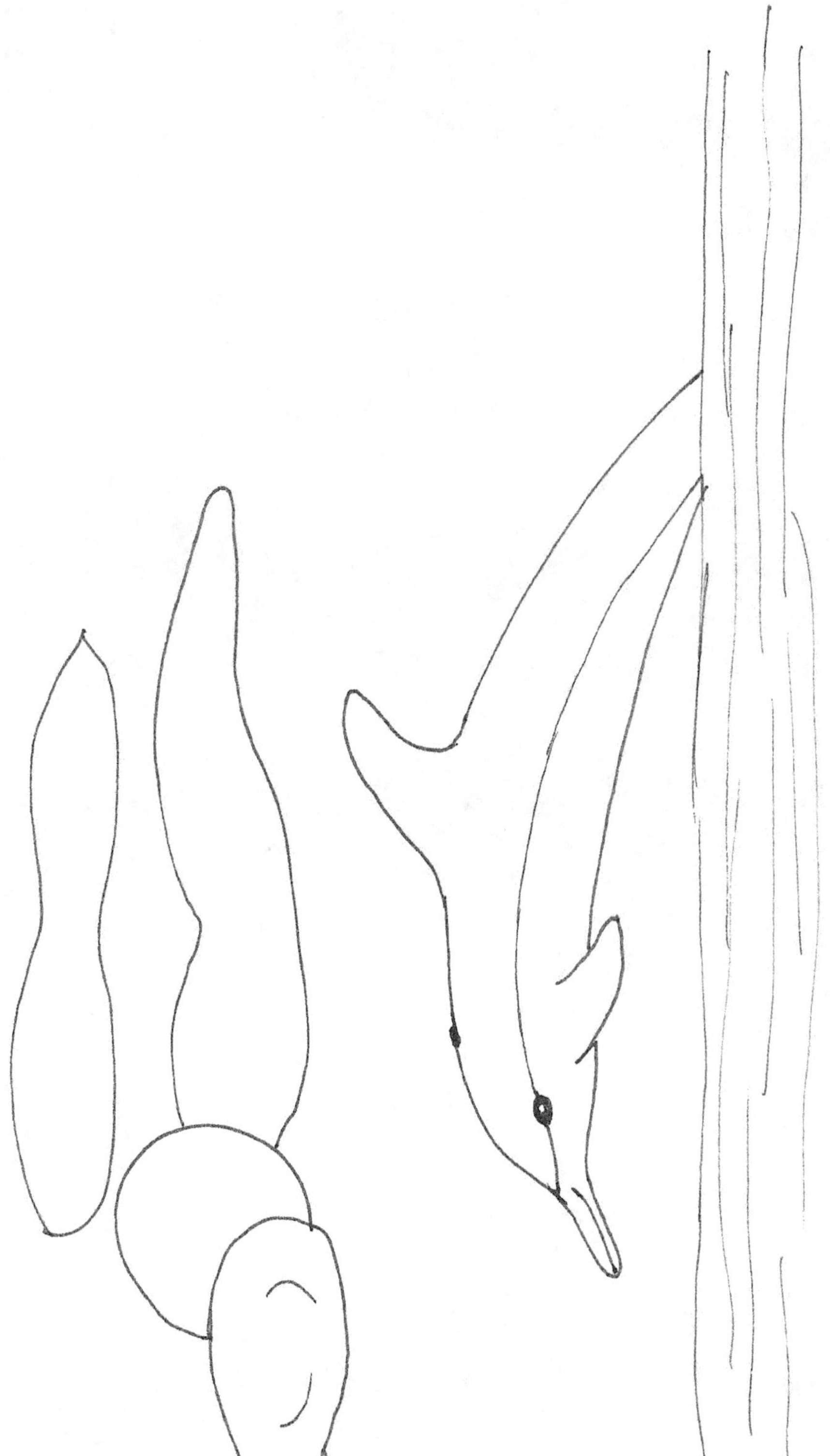

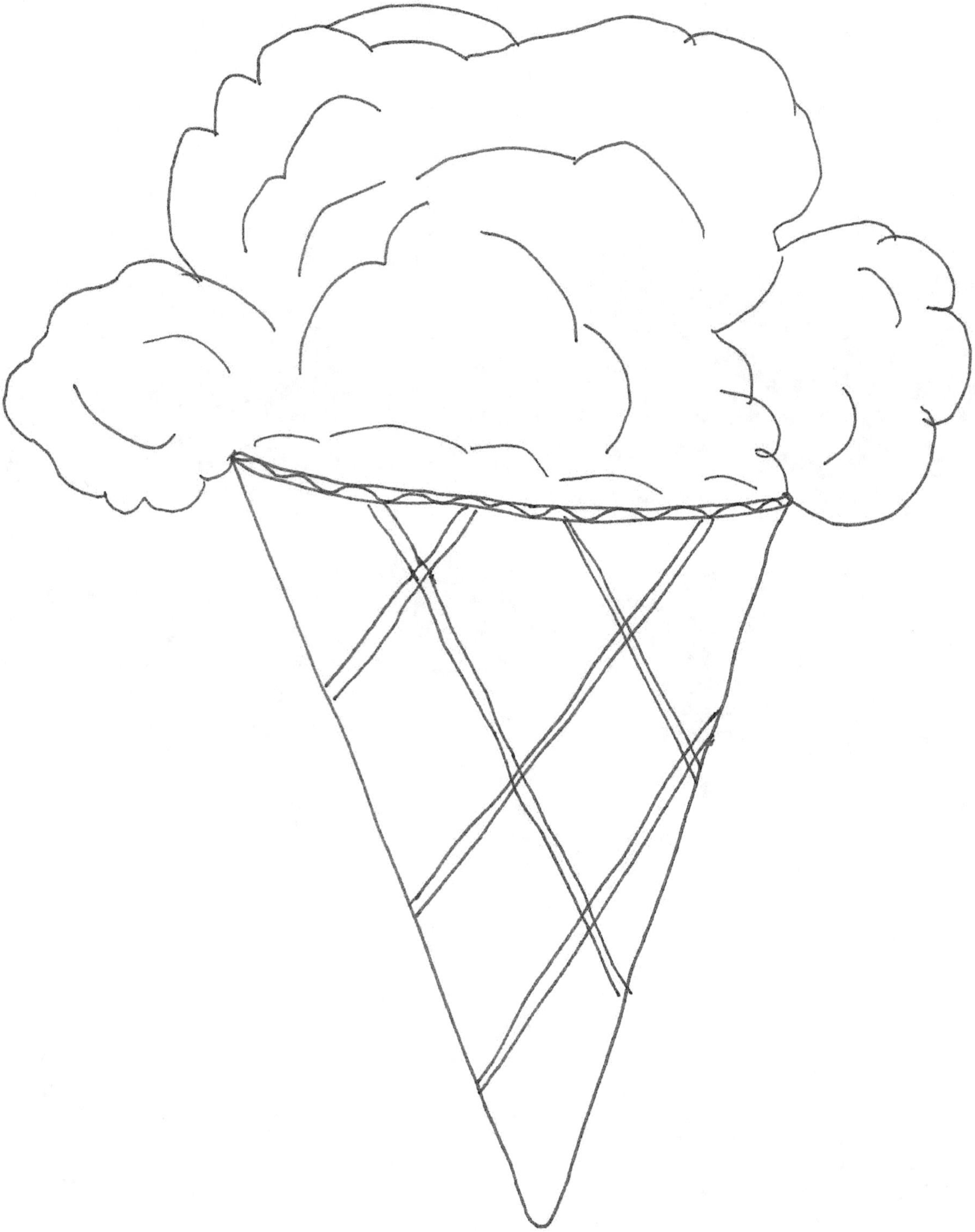

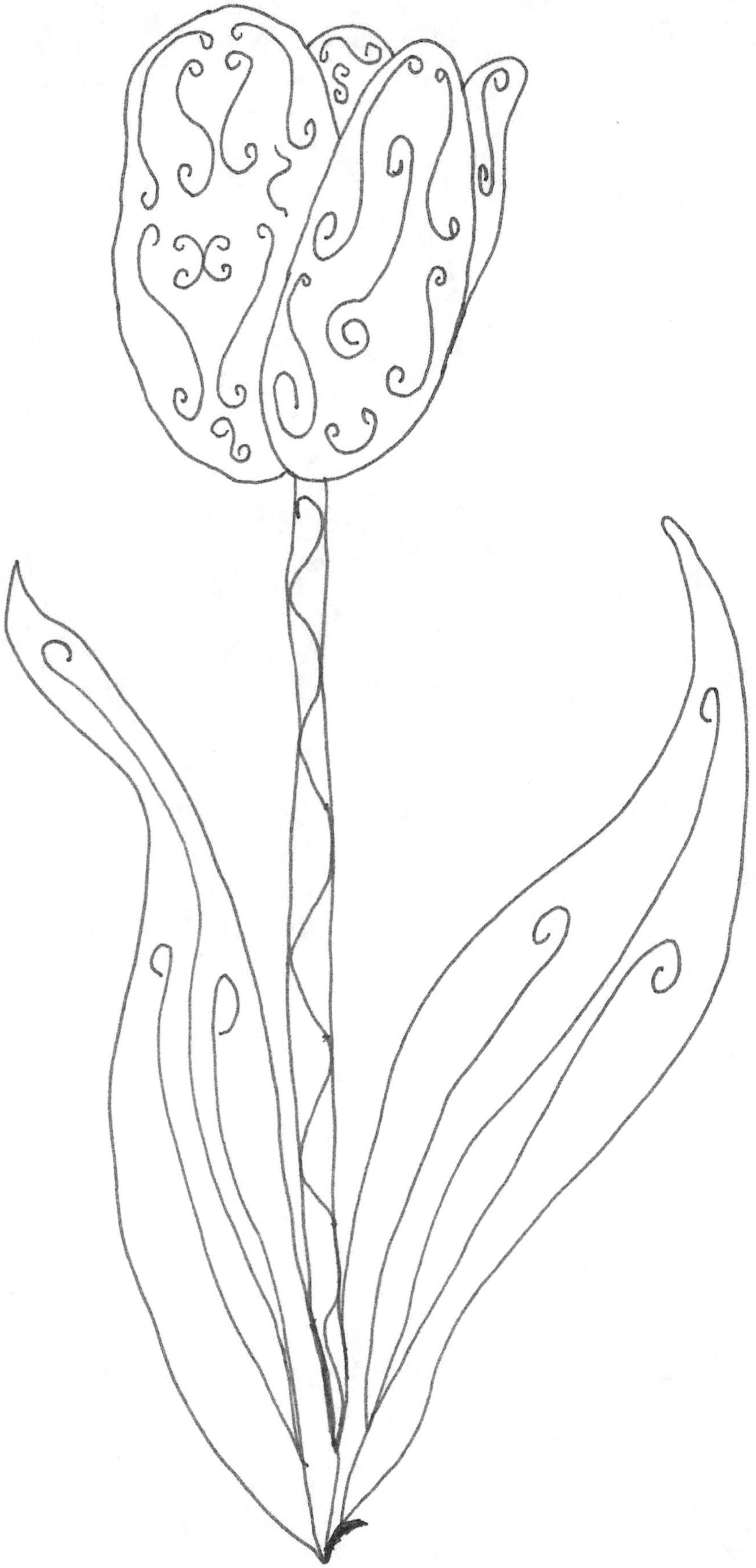

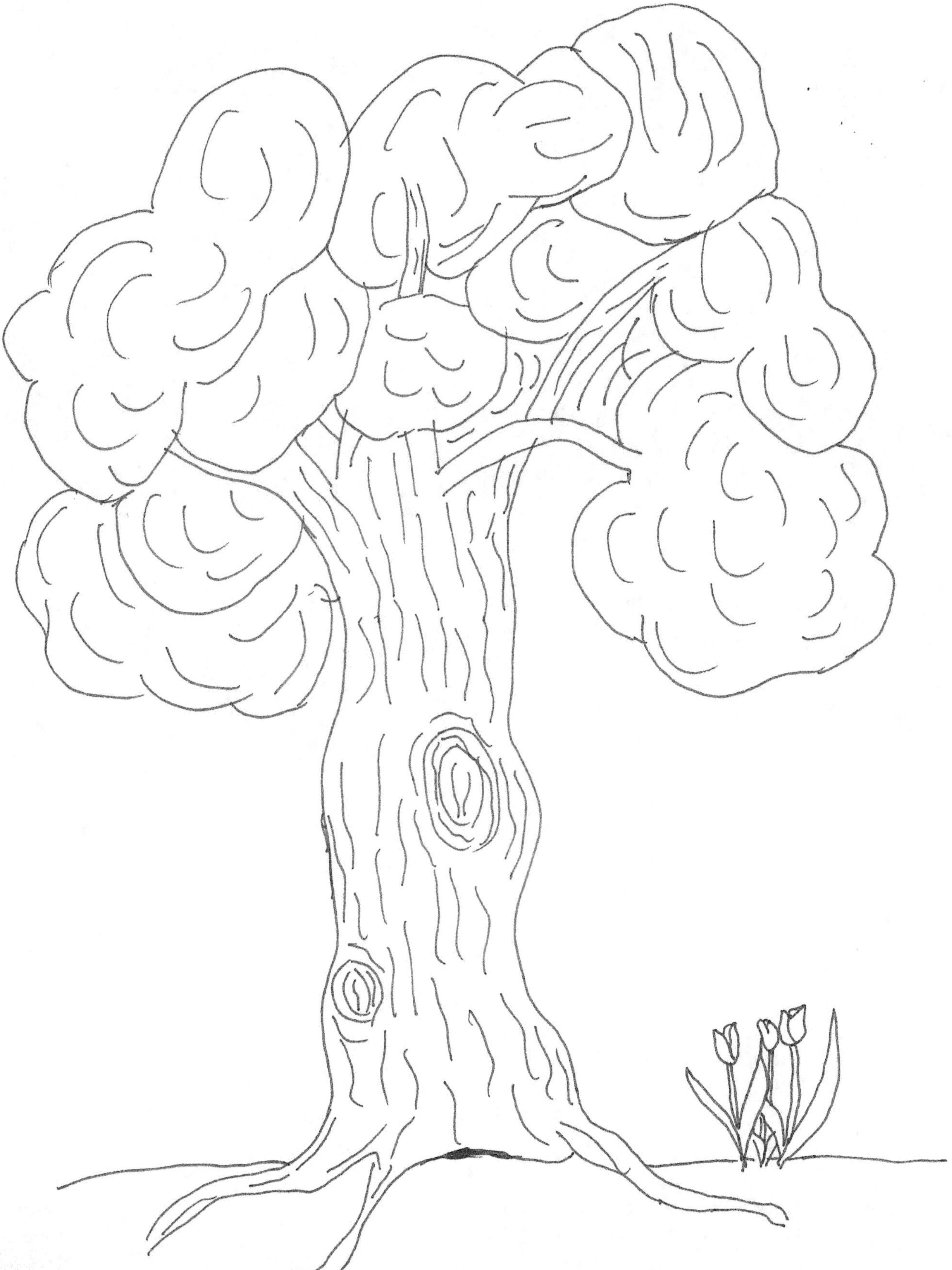

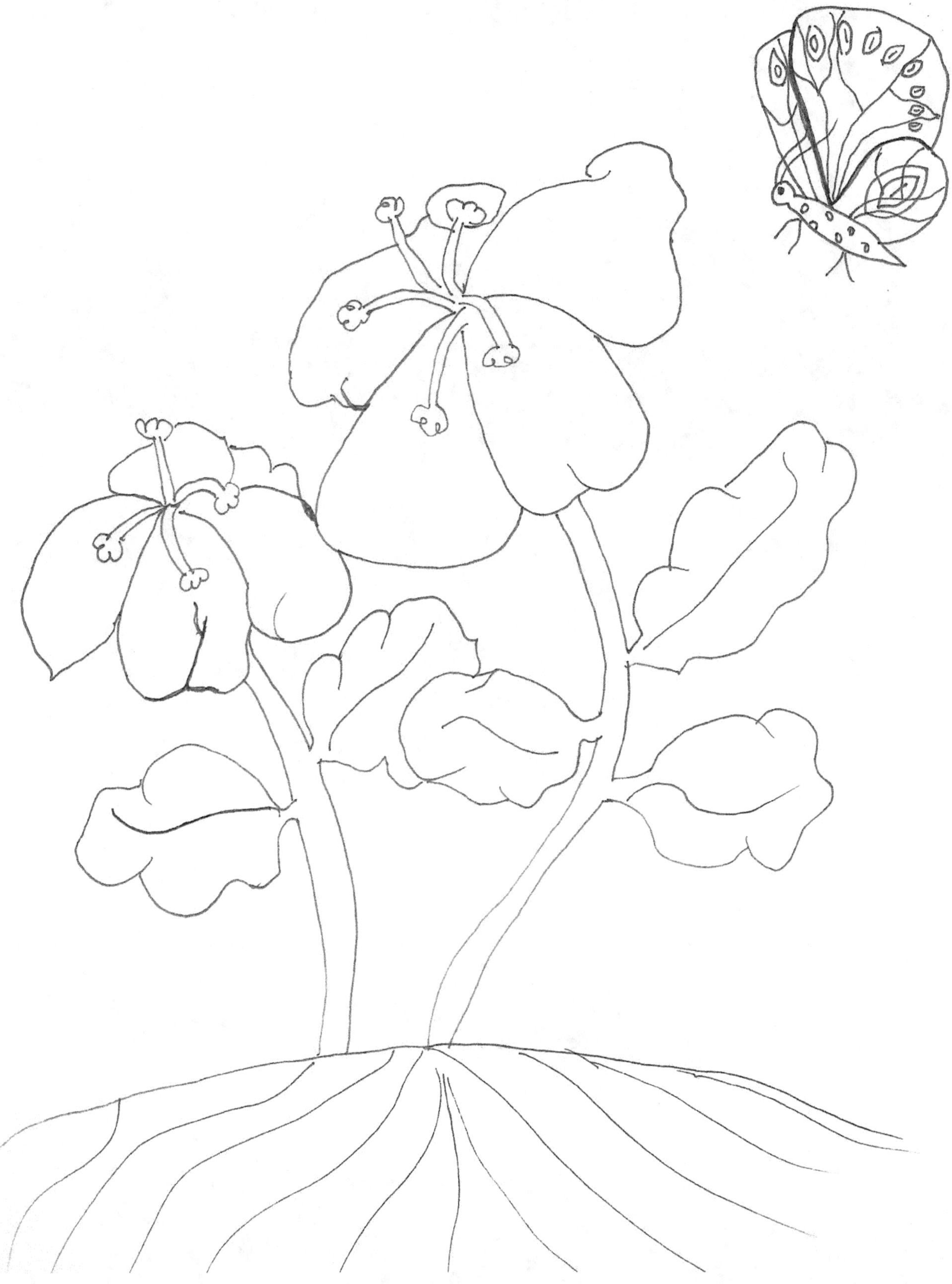

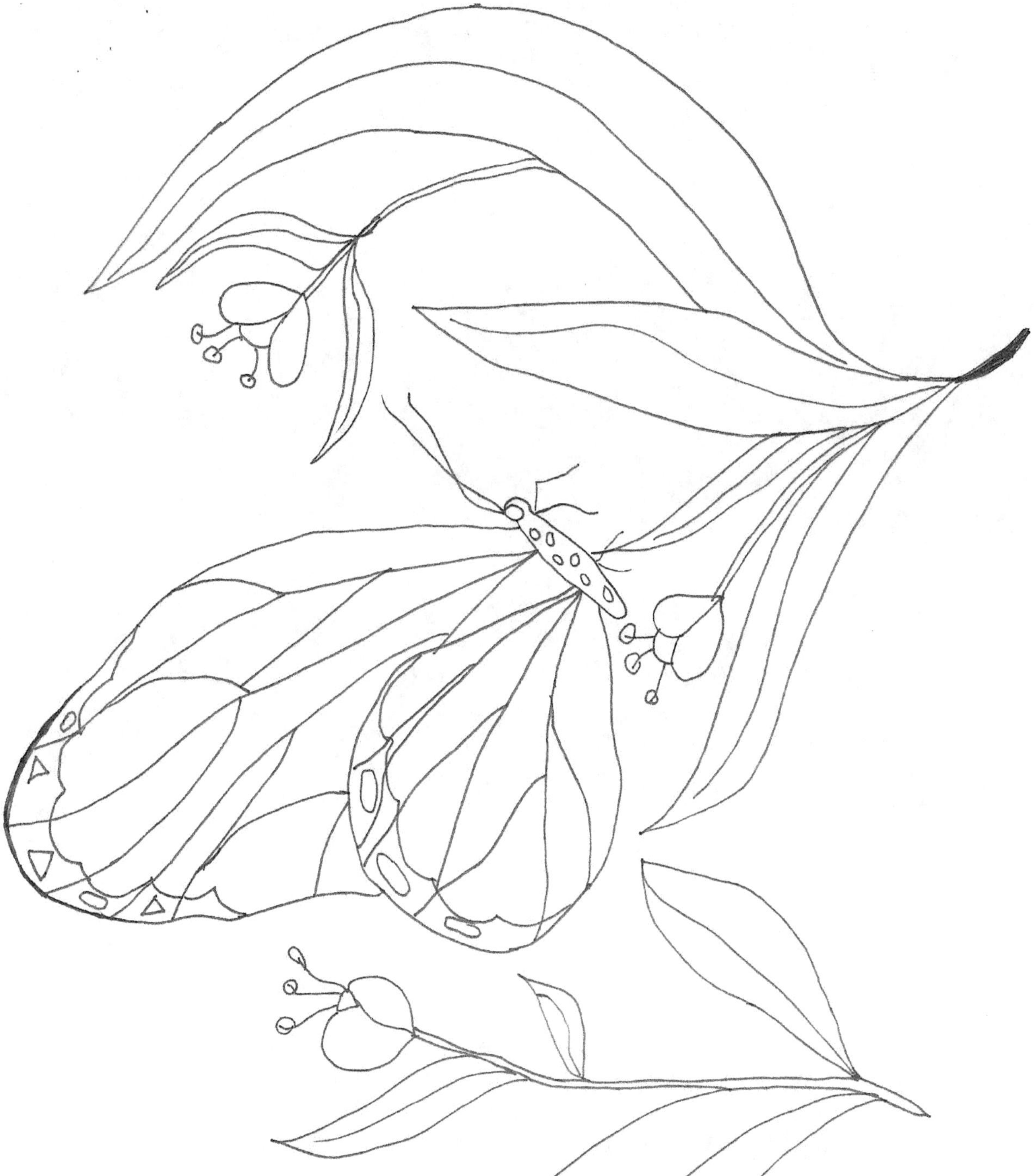

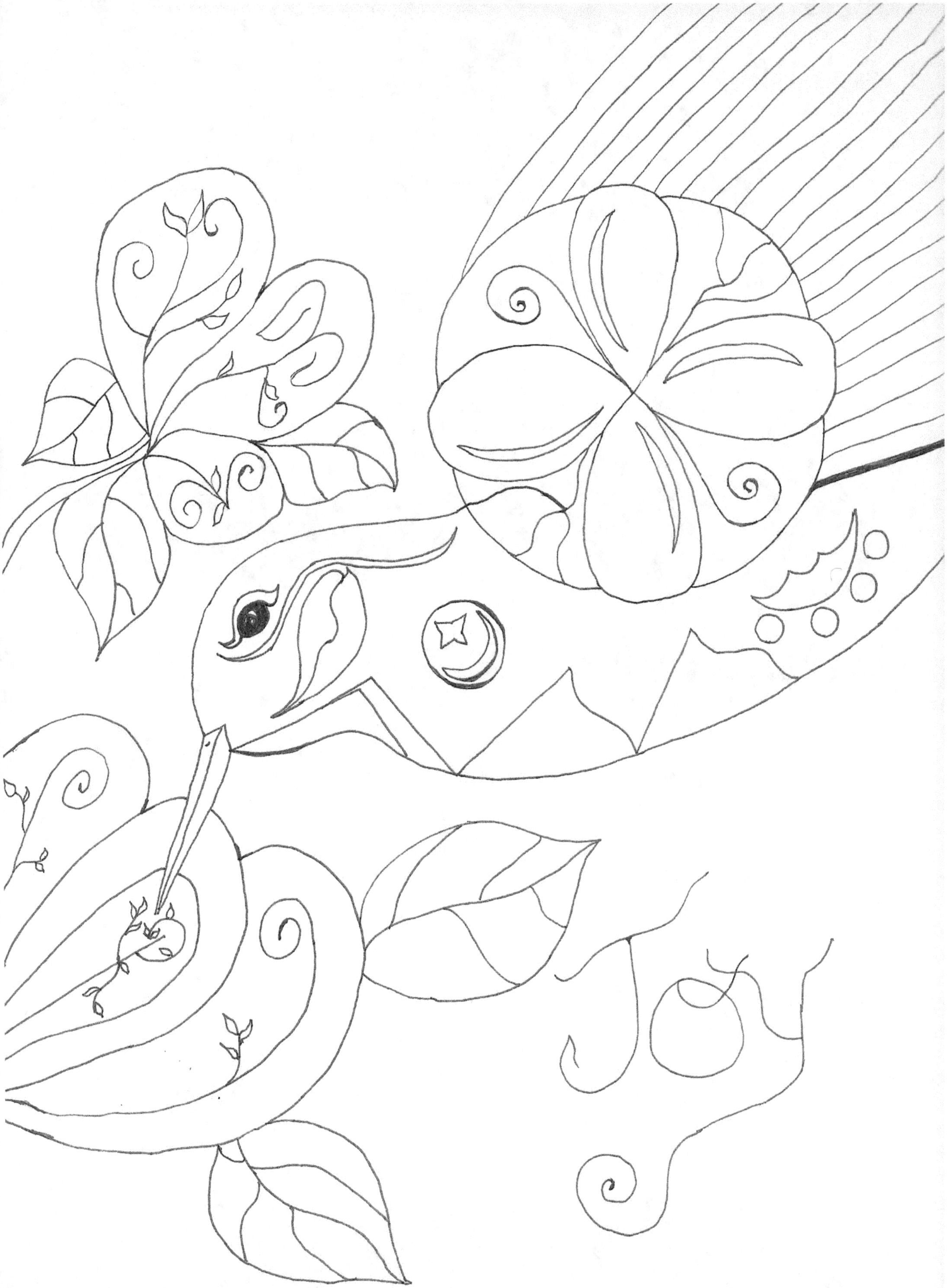
Joy

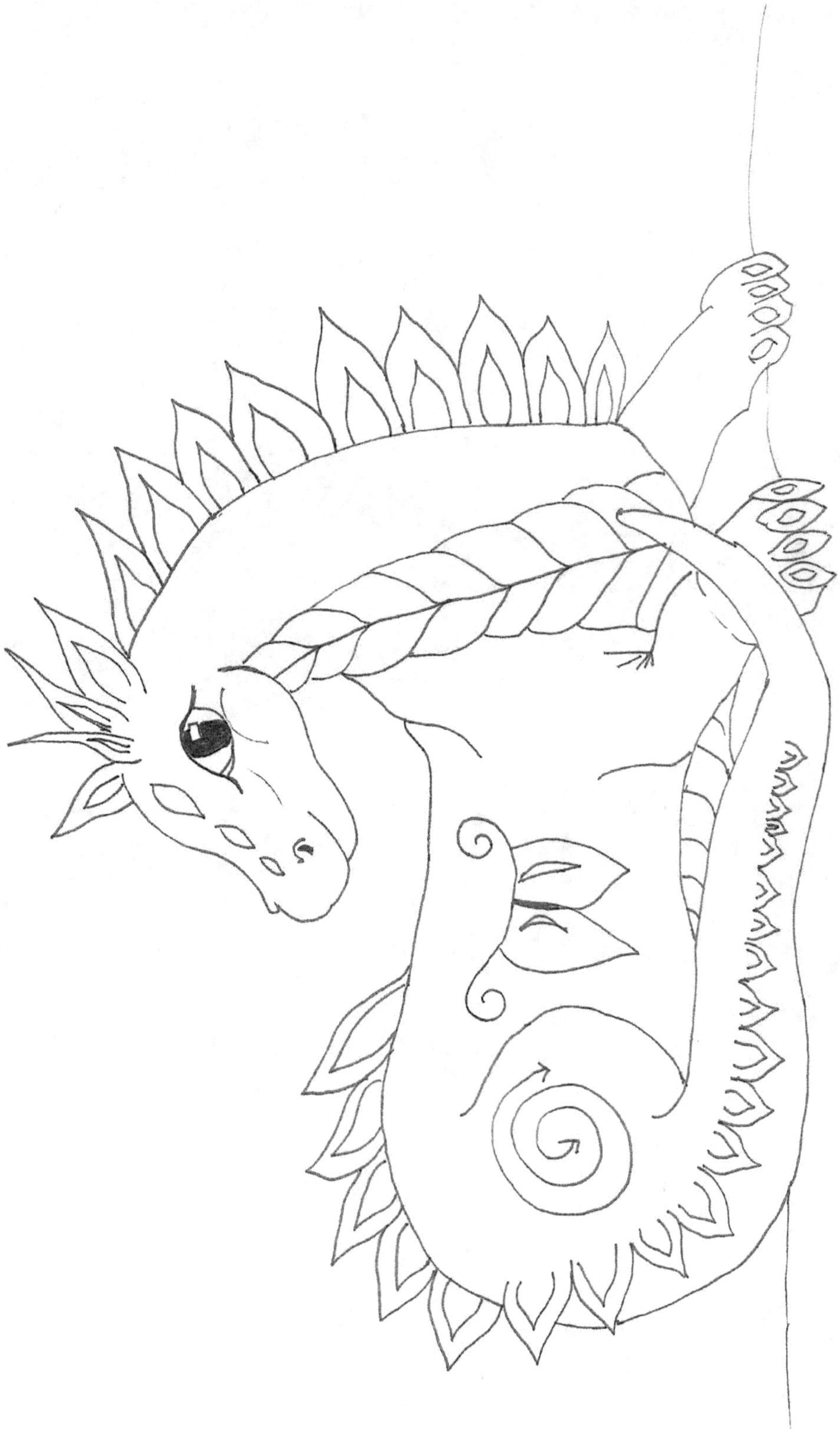

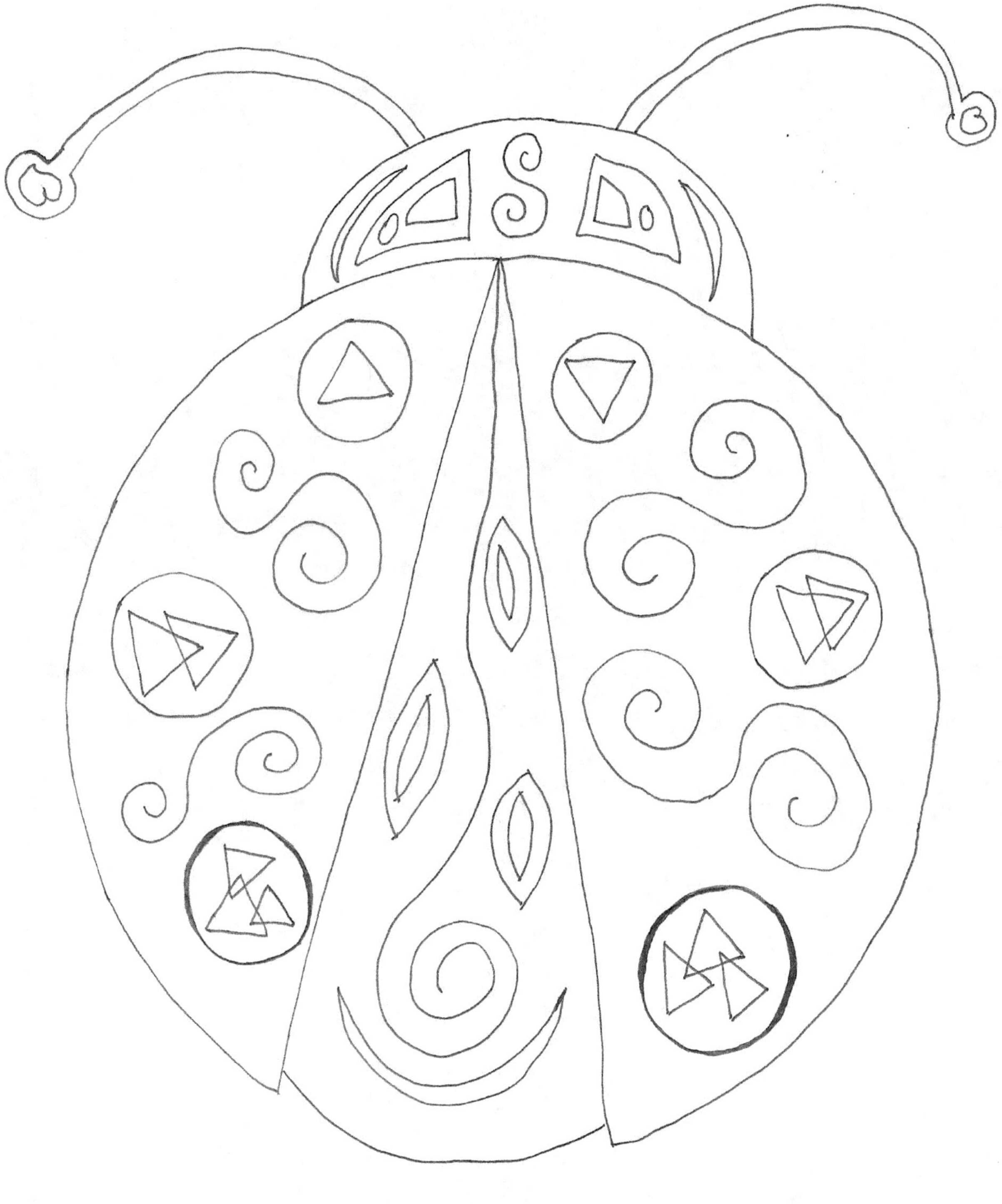

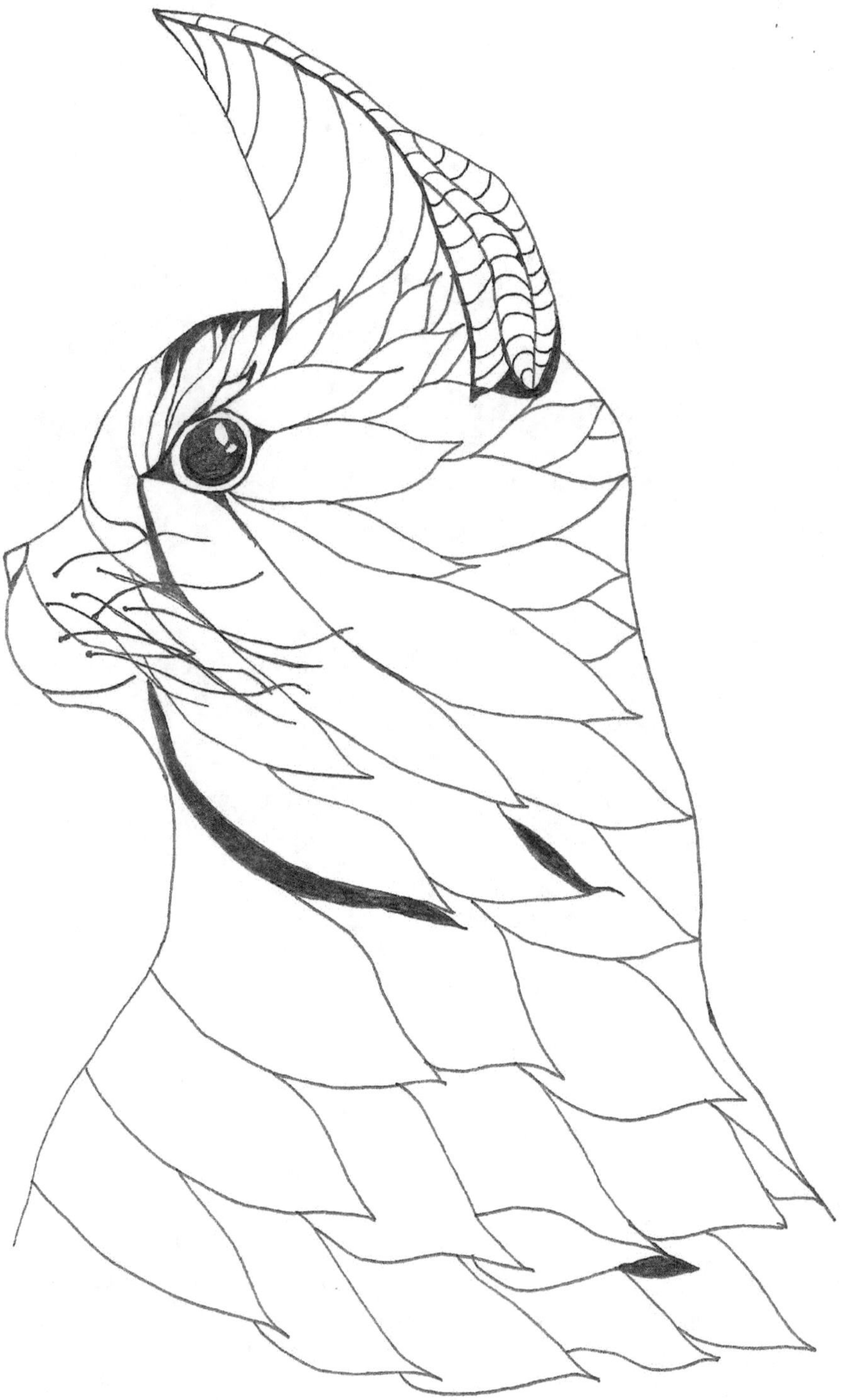

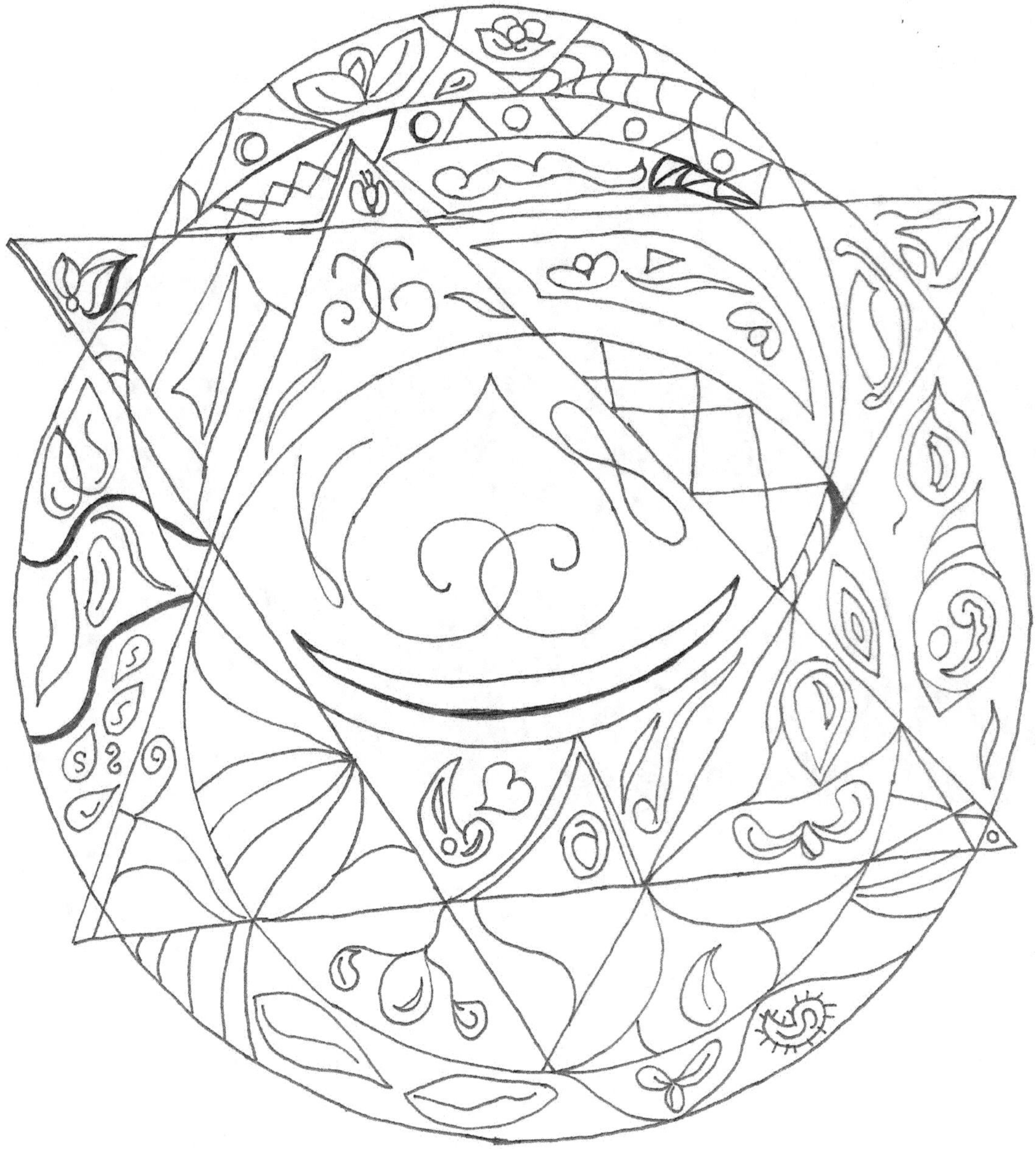

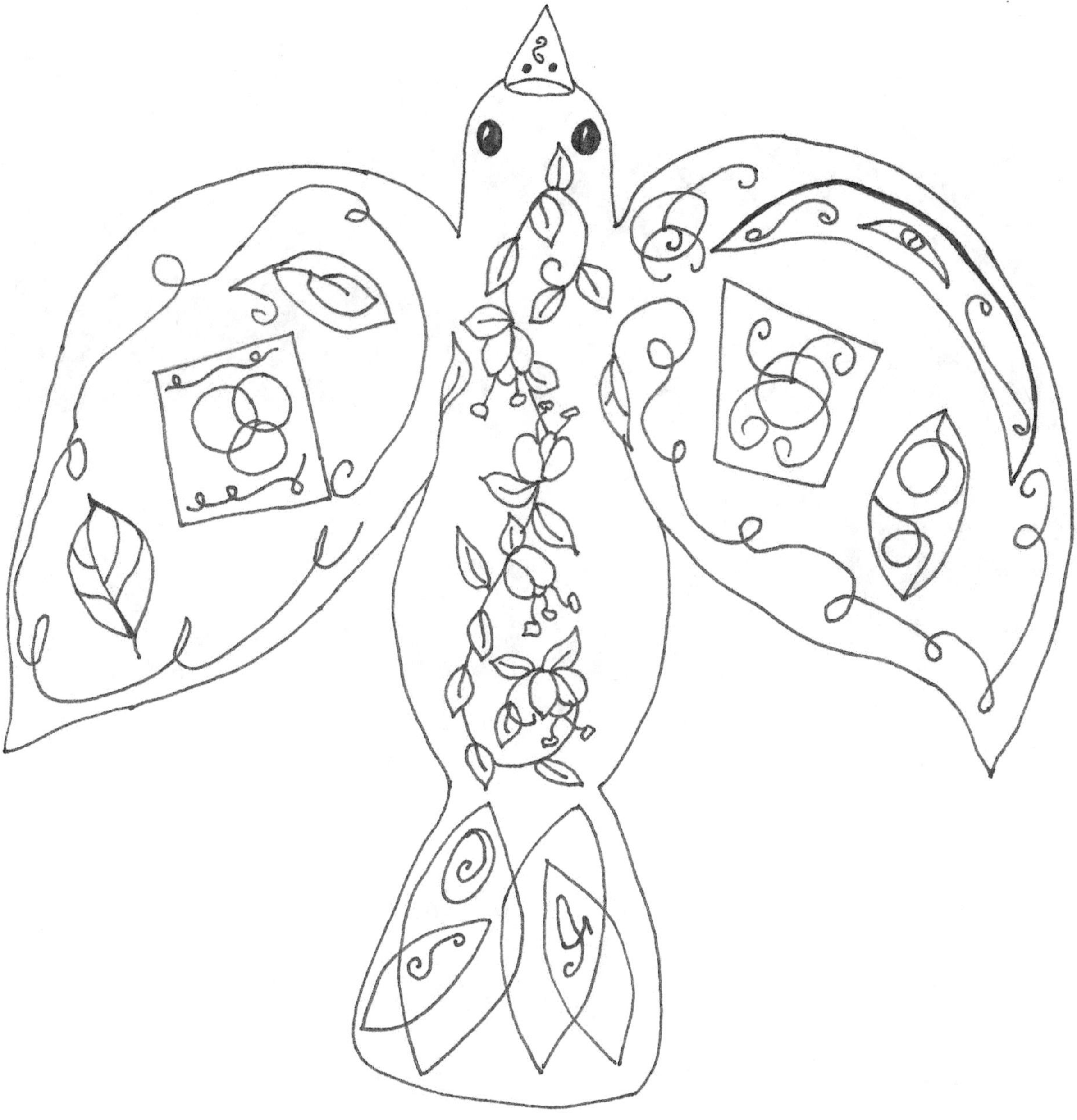

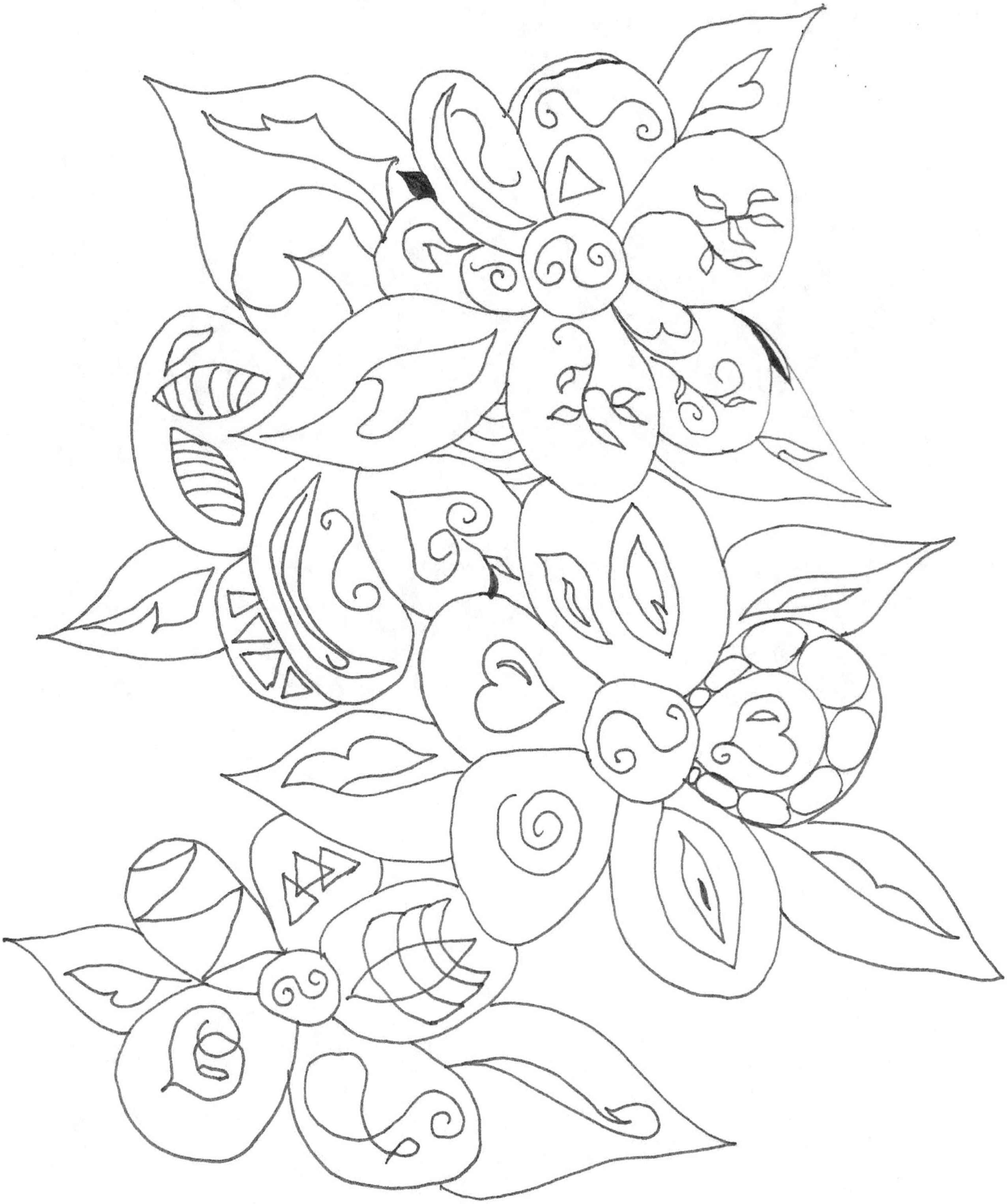

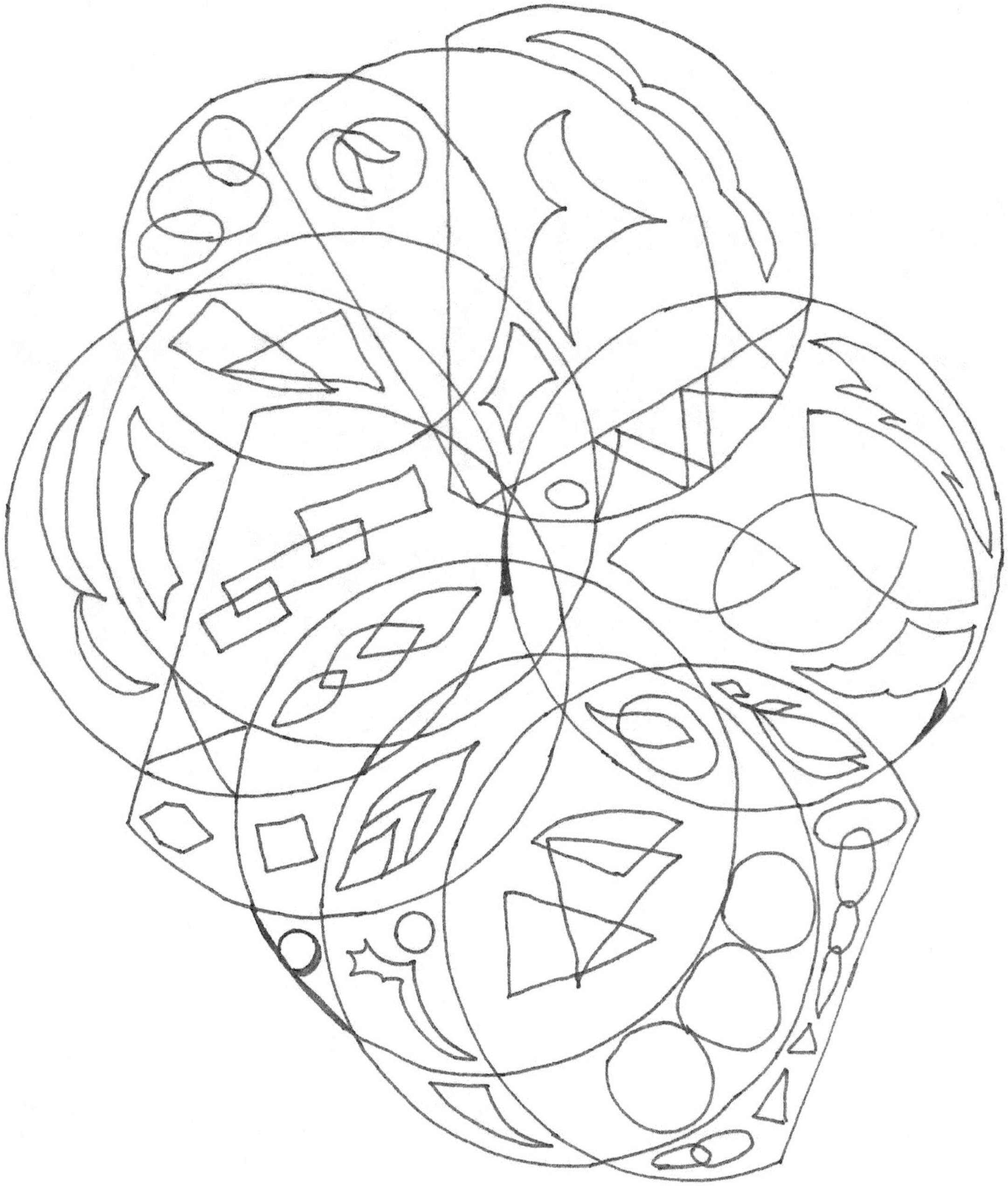

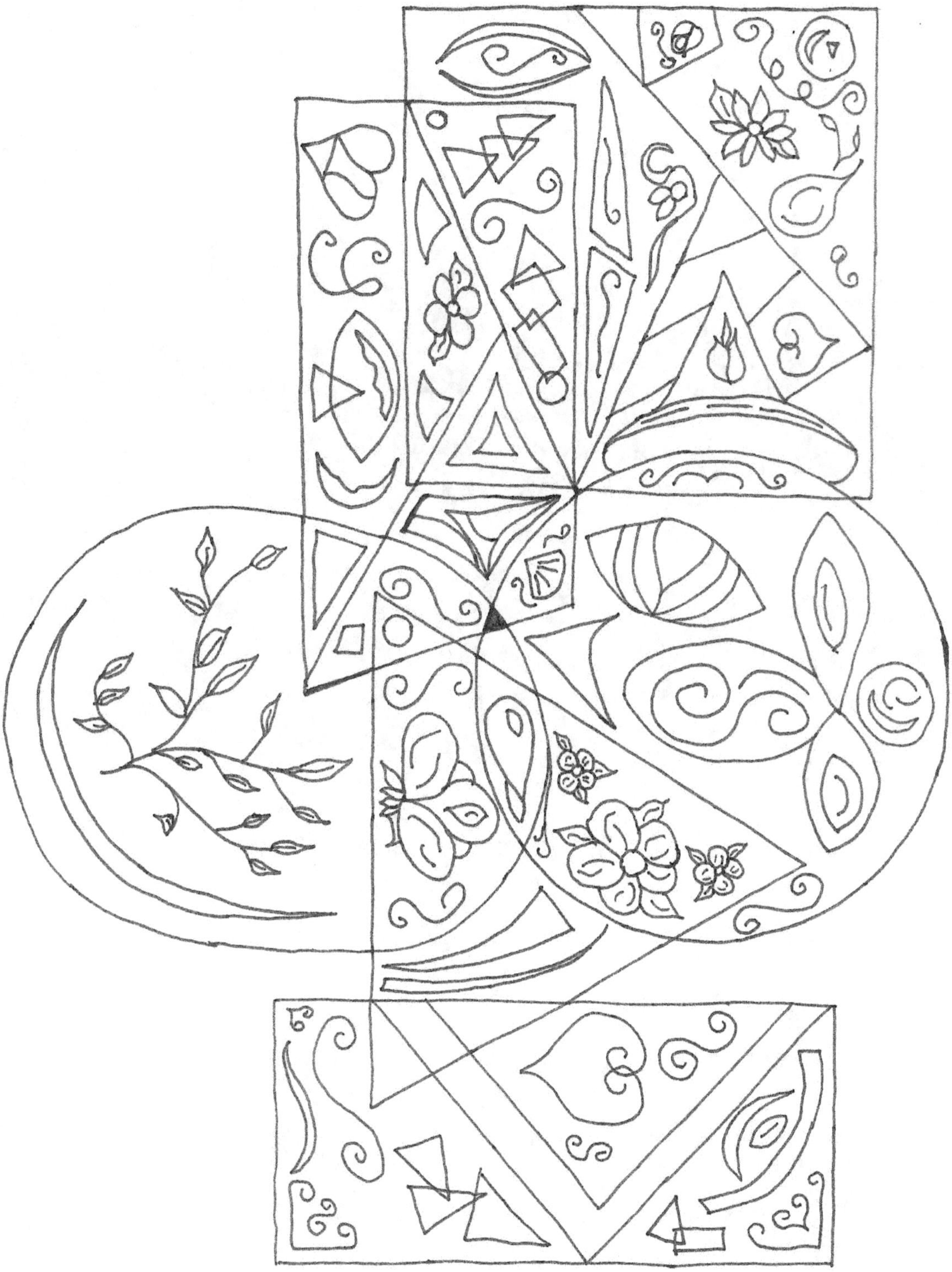

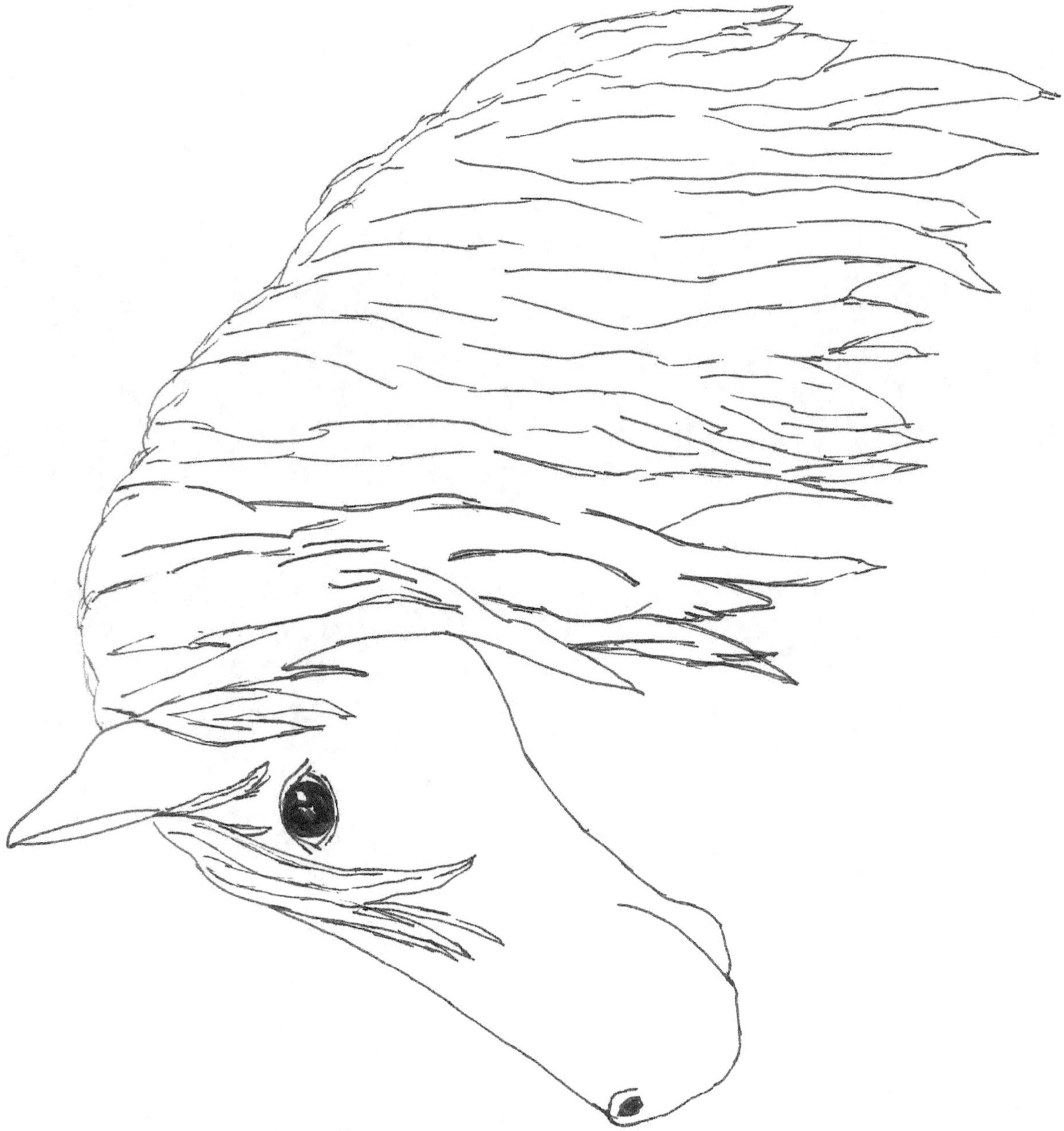

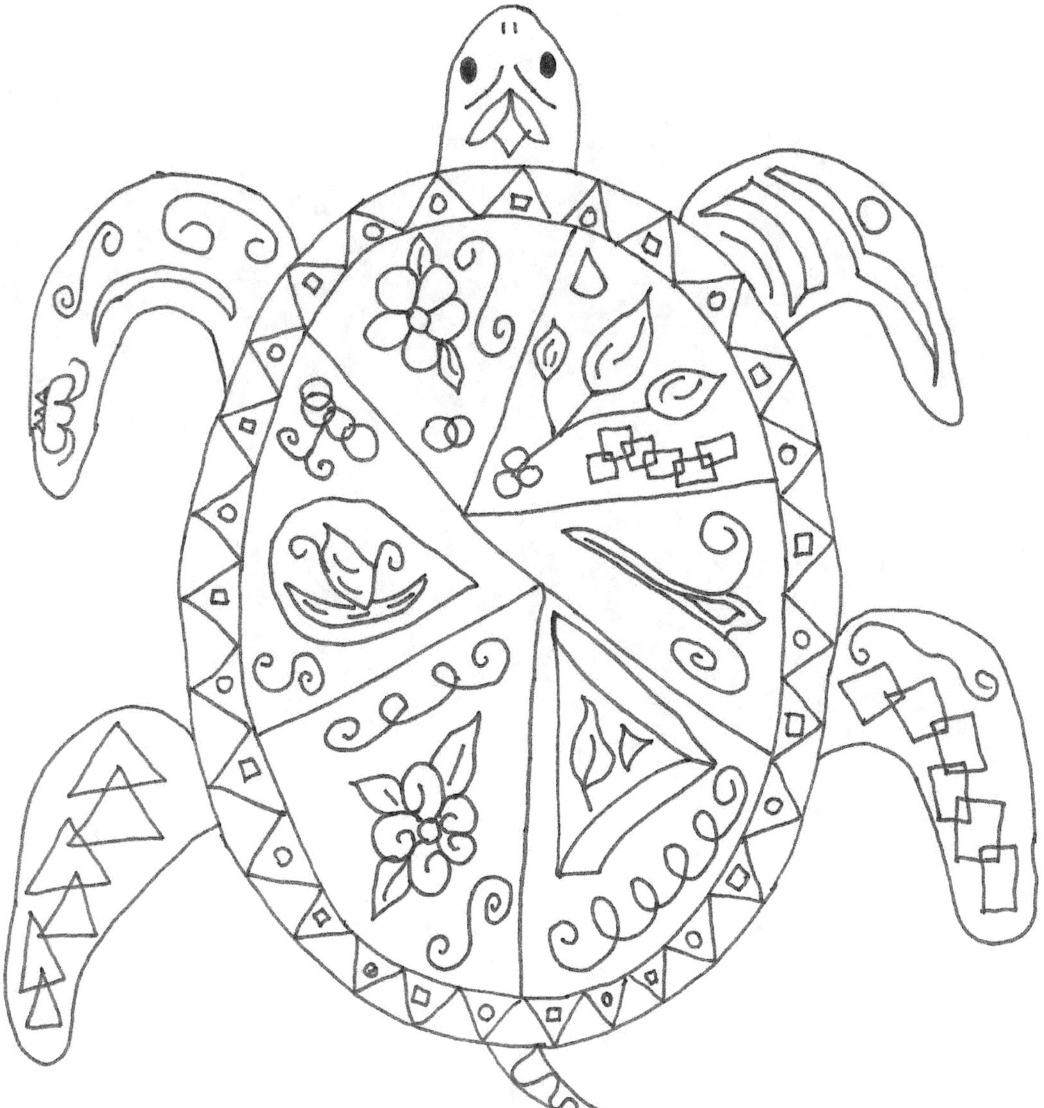

www.ingramcontent.com/pod-product-compliance
Lightning Source LLC
Chambersburg PA
CBHW080849170526
45158CB00009B/2681
* 9 7 8 0 9 8 5 0 0 3 2 3 4 *